Light Airs

Mick Evans

Published by Cinnamon Press
www.cinnamonpress.com

The right of Mick Evans to be identified as author of this work has been asserted by him in accordance with the Copyright, Designs and Patent Act, 1988. © 2021, Mick Evans
ISBN 978-1-78864-109-8

British Library Cataloguing in Publication Data. A CIP record for this book can be obtained from the British Library.

All rights reserved. No part of this publication may be reproduced, stored in a retrieval system, or transmitted in any form or by any means, electronic, mechanical, photocopying, recording or otherwise without the prior written permission of the publishers. This book may not be lent, hired out, resold or otherwise disposed of by way of trade in any form of binding or cover other than that in which it is published, without the prior consent of the publishers.

Designed and typeset in Bodoni by Cinnamon Press. Cover design by Adam Craig © Adam Craig.

Cinnamon Press is represented by Inpress

Acknowledgements

With heartfelt thanks to Jan Fortune for her unstinting encouragement and sensitive guidance, her constant fund of inspiration; for giving so much of herself in the cause of writers and writing. To Adam, for his profound understanding of myth, and his patience with my administrative failures, and for a brilliant cover design beyond my imaginings.
To Jane Belli for her belief and encouragement, and the support of everyone in the Ffynon Wen writers group. To the Dinefwr Poets group, for friendship, support, and exchange of ideas. To all of the above for their kindness, and willingness to share their love of poetry.
And, of course, to Siân, the light and air.

To my family, for the light and the lightness.

Contents

Hymns Ancient and Modern

i. Argonauts	13
ii. the brethren learn to swim	14
iii. spillage	15
iv. Business plan	16
v. Drone	17
vi. November	18
vii. Moldiwarp	19

Why weep ye by the tide, Lady?

End of term	23
Styx	24
Stagecraft	26
The Gardener	28
National Gallery	29
Circe	30
Transit of Venus	31

Breviary

Incipit	35
2 a.m. Vigil	36
The confessional	37
3 a.m. to dawn. Matins	39
Daybreak Lauds	41
First hour of daylight: Prime	42
9 a.m. Terce	44
Commute	45
Noon Sext	46
3 p.m. Nones	49
Sunset Vespers	54
Before retiring Compline	55
Finis	57

Light Airs

Orpheus in the underpass	61
Fire on Saddleworth	62
Girl arranging bananas	63
The uses of avocado	64
Inkling	66
Dawn chorus cadenza	68
Lammas	70
Angelus	71
Presences	74
The miller's tale	75
The molluscs on theology	78
Light airs	80
Chopstick variations	82
Triple point	85
To learn	88

Light Airs

discovering a thief in his cell
and desirous to be less of the world
Macarius helped the man load his donkey
with all his remaining belongings
vegetables from his plot
his last blanket his bowl

I would hear the donkey's opinion

Hymns Ancient and Modern

i. argonauts

From here currents will drift you westward.
Some of you may survive;
others will be spared more suffering.

All moneys are in safe keeping.
Do not expect to be welcome:
tolerance is sufficient.

Find space away from recollection and sight of home:
this is for the best.
Nowhere is left for hope of return

Future generations may construct myths of your journey.
This is no concern of ours.
Forget any who seek to help or harm you.

There is little water, less food:
fasting is needful at the birth of religions.
From now   you're on your own.

ii. The brethren learn to swim

For the sisters banished to the rock
desertion is anathema
Let us make sacraments of veniality

At midnight towards redemption
under the hag of the breasts
who acknowledges our suffering

address the path familiar to us
On the street of the dead
our sandals' leather will not betray intent

secrete the pallor of starved faces
beneath the cowl of austerity
Labour under the moon's attraction

At the shoreline cast off our habits
as for an oblation
Celebrate the justification of faith

Trust in holy writ
for Peter walked on water
until he feared

the sisters' warm breath
will dry salt crust on our skin
their laughter overwhelm damnation

Strike out for deliverance
in each thrust against the tide
until we feel broken shells beneath our feet

and among the rocks know ourselves men
From that fertile shore the call to matins will quicken us
the coarse wool of our faith restored

Comfort our sisters in their exile
For this much of eternity
we may be forgiven

iii. Spillage

past sight of land
the hair of young girls
floating fan-like on the current

drifts of flowers
among orange lifejackets
and empty water bottles

the bloated bodies will be searched for abuse
latex fingers probe for scarring
each distended vulva a Sheena na Gig

Colmcille in his cell stands to greet a visitor
whose loose cloak will upturn the ink
flooding a month's toil

raising orisons for careless souls

iv. Business plan

Of course they have language
but you don't want to listen too closely.
Or learn it.

Over the years
who could face so many appeals
and keep sane?

Often just the expression:
avoiding eye contact is the issue.
A useful trick.

Most nights I slept well.
But trust me, this is better. Cleaner. More efficient.
A case of practical economics

on both sides: our means, their ends.
Go easy with that fuel. It costs.
You can start the engine now.

A perfect night. It's grey out there.
Such a romantic term, white horses.
Help to shove them off; it's near closing time.

Funny, but at this point
I always think of Bleriot's question:
arms waving in the general direction.

And in whatever language one cares to choose
or they might understand, the usual advice:
Arbeit macht frei

v. Drone

Public information memo.

Be assured that the safety and well-being
of all our military personnel is paramount.

With access to the highest levels of technology
and years of rigorous training, we honour their service;

We are committed to demonstrating consideration and care
and achieving positive outcomes for them in all situations.

As Investors in People we recognise
they are our greatest asset in maintaining national security.

As a consequence, it has been decided
all future casualties of conflict will be of non-combatant status.

New treaties have been signed and procedures already developed
and thoroughly tested on lesser countries.

Our allies as well as all potential enemies
are in full agreement with this new accord.

To this end, major departments have been tasked
with the refinement of the art of collateral damage.

There will naturally be a rigorous
and entirely unbiased random selection process.

Soon we will have the perfect solution
coming through a window near you.

vi. November

The Butcher, the Baker, the Candlestick Maker...

Stretched on the wire one saw red meat
One saw how they went down like wheat
And one lit their path to the mercy seat

Which finding empty
They understood defeat

vii. Moldiwarp

another world haunts him
will uncoil his guts for augury
to scorch and harden under circling crows

skin his pulsing flesh
to poultice on goitres
pocket his severed hands secrete his torso

with cobwebs in kitchen corners
muslin-bagged
neutralise his stench

listening in plays the innocent
lurking in the draughts
of their passing

he hears rumours
of vastnesses below his world
worked by demons who make garments of his skin

he's dark matter
dirt in his nails convicts him
his kind's not natural

sifting dust
in the charnel
subverting landscapes

futures root him up
earth's chagrin their slops
unroof his dark world

prise apart his galleries
he'll suffer their whispers
Mehr licht

dig deeper

Why weep ye by the tide, Lady?

End of term

when I think of you now it is of first and last things
arriving for work once and the smell of alcohol
and that it did not seem to matter

and that last conversation when you still knew how to be happy
a small house you said
enough money to get you to the campsite in Brittany

how finally we came to understand one another
when we both confessed
to dreading those warm up sessions in drama

how in the end they always came down to
having to trust someone
reaching out
touch

Styx

batte col remo qualunque s'adagia, *(he beats with an oar any who delay)*
Inferno Canto 3, 111

Your business here
in default of authority or ceremony
I would know you without artifice

First in this realm is nakedness
Cast off your blue dress
This rag billowing of oceans

Bare the limbs' remnants the tattered flesh
the gore of crab and dogfish
unclasp your fingers' adornments

The worth of such is known here
where is no brightness
                        Speak

The oar upon your shoulder will find its proper use
my rings that they know me
after disfigurement of claw and pincer

I swam into the sun's decline
beyond detritus and grey wash of tide
corrupt until the current took me

a covenant of elements shedding strata
a cracked amphora
spilling red wine

should I recall the fertile slopes
my feet unblemished in cool grass
not fearing the scorpion's spur

or the fractured mirror
the sands' fossil ribs
hoar frosted salt bloomed

to dream again in rifted mosaics
of falling through the cracks
Their shards scar me

At the shoreline to form discarded shells into creatures
for the tide's reach the moon's draw
back to imagined dwellings

This much was easy
But daily to drag the choking from the surf
Feel bone through blankets and shroud the dead

From the hum of flies
stench of bloated drowned
I have studied to spurn siren voices

the lark's song fading
'And I on a soft pillow
Will lay down my limbs'

This testimony of brands and scars
claw of waves on cliffs you make an anthem

Will you endure deprivation
of the cool shadow of Olympus
the grape and piquant olive   chestnut and pine

the hot springs' rise within your loins each morning
at evening the lyre
                      Be certain
for here you find no myth of return

no fellowship
touch of flesh and scented groves
grief must be voiceless

at last consent
to absent but not absolve the self

'and look upon the lotus banks'
is why I come

Your coin

Stagecraft

A descent

under the lighting gantry
waiting to prop the ladder
till she was clear

her noli me tangere
stalled intrusion
from apex to root

a shadow glimpsed
from terra firma
shifting through the whole array

in cognition of a private art
fine adjustment and modulation
to make the spectrum split apart

Syrinx

after four rehearsals she got it right
the desperate flight to the water's edge
overwhelming need   widening ripples

from beyond the rushlights
haunting song of voices pleading
implacable sense of clawing hands

then the lost days
a beach find of beads and gems

of this pale reed little remaining

deus ex machina

artistically frowned upon
a sign of authorial exhaustion
a contrivance
intervention by external force or circumstance
a dramatic device
emerging at the crisis
figured by the moral quality of the protagonist
but independent of all other action
or
when all else fails
an intercession
a last resort
a Salve Regina
a resolution
a way out

exit via two haiku

last trip through the town
shops' yellow glare and dazzle
a descent through days

until waves enfold
and light falls differently
on old enactments

The Gardener

Saahirah, I wish you joy of your garden
its streams and rich fruits
and divisions for peace and contemplation

On the breeze the scent of oranges
Through vaulted arches
your delicate fingers will train the vine

Between temperate arcades and terraces
formulate original quadrants
where pools reflect the shade of myrtles

This enclosed space of seasons
will ripen the pomegranate
the kumquat to freshen the tongue

I think of you journeying in cool mornings
to bathe in the rivers
hair spread on kindly water

stretching your limbs and taking ease
Birdsong shall accompany your steps
the precession of planets your entertainment

Do not forget us
Observe tenderly the green shoot the full leaf
Number the infinity of pebbles

You have time

National Gallery

Oi Oi Saveloy!
              night fugitives
bear the weight of their fallen
snapped stiletto dangling
What Maides will you light a Candell
seven figures in a wooden boat aground in Spitalfields
find refuge
            and the belles of Shoreditch
transcendent at angelwings on brick
may yet safely regain
immaculate and intact
(Matt has herpes
Beigels all night
I found the dancing awkward)
Brick Lane
            and gates of Troy

Circe

at the beach cafe the bronzed waitress in denims
curls her tattoos and flirts with a blond youth
single handed texts orders to the bar
is uninterested in producing our bill
her naked omphalos focuses the world
as evening falls

we have crossed oceans
for dust music and sangria
now at the tide turn
honouring old gods and finding the evening cool
should we make libations to the red sky
driftwood fire and white tipped breakers
gather rich woven blankets about us and sleep under stars
dreaming the roasted ox the lyre
powers to suppress the winds

the couple at a corner table begin to argue
he is angry she cannot remember some detail important to him
from the history of their love
she tries and tries
eventually she gives up and leaves
he does not follow her
in cold blue light of a full moon she will shear close her hair
and let the tears run down her cheeks

I make vows
tonight I will caress your ridged scar
a seam that stitched you back to life
tomorrow we must cross the lands where Homer sang for bread
and after this his wine-dark sea

Transit of Venus

there's a wedding and you have a new dress
chance purchase online
a rarity in midnight blue

straight from packaging you shake out creases
try its full length
you are delighted to fit it so well

your curves emphasised but demure
you require help with the zip
which reaches from nape to buttocks

do not believe I am not tempted
after the fitting
you slip off to change

in two minutes
a not entirely guiltless voyeur
I catch your flash in the mirror

though a predictable phenomenon
our orbits unite in only occasional commensurabilities
crossing briefly

what seems to observers a caress
tracks self conscious separation
fading to embarrassment

like the morning you ran in from the shower naked
—sublimate that to nude—
towel clutching thinking the coast clear

I try to remember last encounters
thinking of remote events
Sorry you said

Breviary

Incipit

paean

it's serious now
this requirement of growing old
needing to apologise
asking people to repeat themselves
seeing them roll their eyes
and bits of worn carcass getting lost
or breaking down

and girls at the checkout saying Sweetheart
well that's something
because I pose no threat
or interest

when my father died
going through his wallet and finding his bus pass
his face in its little plastic window
and my telephone number in biro on a scrap of paper
for someone else to find
or a talisman
afraid he would be unable to recall it one day
on an unrecognisable street

wondering how soon before *Past it*
becomes the description of choice
and whether I'll be able to bear
the weight of it
the responsibility of remembering
and it just getting more
bloody
pain in the arse difficult
the light of the world

2 a.m. Vigil

Miserere mei

Junk
My sweet friend,
Do you want to see me fling naked, without robe.
I will dance only for you, baby.

Wondering
          Are you real
or only my chief suspect
thick-fingered internet ghoul
hunting credit cards
                      but
if true Salome
how exactly you just might *fling*
without robe

Where did you learn that word for joy
but also shame

Perhaps you were dictated to
That also is bad grammar

Over distances doors slam
A windowless van deposits girls on corners
After beatings threats are enough

Sweet gods free this slave

Tonight I lie awake for wrong reasons

As perhaps do you.

The confessional

soothsayer

Vampire-like I avoid reflection
The mirror knows too many secrets
I stay ambivalent

The one who looks you in the eye
never tells you straight
about important things like that handful of sand

I have watched you through too many moments
indecisions or plain bad ones
into the grey truth of morning

or waiting for mail that does not come
a weighing of promises
a book of revelation
paper thin and easily burned

Confession requires a particular kind of concealment
By now I'm getting to know how it's going to be
Who'll win, who lose, whose blood I'll drink
Who I'll let down

Only with so much to give away
I'm not telling

Eyeful

Blocking off the good eye cured my childhood squint
Pink sticking plaster on metal specs
Lazy eye the doctors said, only my mother got it wrong and called it wandering
        But she was right after all
For hours every fortnight I stalked the pretty nurses
trailed clicking heels down corridors
and stored up fantasies
Shutting down the better side means something goes awry
Half blind and skewed through peripheries
what you think you see is rarely what you get

Shelf life

Last shift: Time, the manager told him,
to keep that promise of shelves she'd asked for over the years.
Coming from the warehouse he'd no inclination
for drilling holes, fixing brackets, and sandpapering;
He'd rather tinker with his trains. She kept asking.
This was how they tested each other's patience.

But it wasn't that that wore down his defence.
One Sunday morning saw the job done:
Planks neatly glossed, between trips to her chair
where she watched new-weeded beds.
By then she was too weak to reach up
with last year's preserves, or balance the anniversary plate.
So when she finally checked out there was plenty of room for guilt.

A fall

No matter how often we put him straight
He'd trot it out: How fallen are the mighty
We'd cackle behind his back
But there's something in that version-
How far and deep the fall
and how exactly we're taken down

My efforts to improve the wisdoms of his age
seem fruitless now. Or arrogant.
Meaning well is what counts
He never got Milton or Ozymandias in his backstreet class
but clung on. Grant me his dignity as I fall from grace

3 a.m. to dawn.   Matins

The owl patrols its silence
The fox rakes out takeaway trays and tampons
Nothing is over yet

Our ghosts meet us halfway
groping towards dawn
insistent on being heard

Hour of unreason
when prayer is furthest
breath shallow
each word a pebble
rosaries of stone

Wrong turns through traffic
By the time I reached the ward he was unconscious
He died believing he was alone

Between the graves
the tenure of identical marble
among the many ways to be lost

Lord
Let there be light

The Larkin thing.

Bought experience is the best, my boy,
As long as
              One of my grandmother's better ones.

Watching from the platform, her window stayed closed,
my waves unreturned; well, there was rain.
A starving leech, I clung on
to something that should have finished sooner.
We didn't meet again.
Later in the bogs I avoided the graffiti on the wall.
A letter came. On first sight
I misread it and thought everything forgiven, after all.
But a closer look yielded words that burned:

After our disagreement how nice to see
you miss your train to make sure
YOU were all right

Home truths sting: arrested development maybe.
What keeps me awake half the night
grips and thickens like glacial ice.
Some things are bought at too high a price.

Feedback

They asked me to wait
after they called in the successful candidate
I chewed my nails and hoped for *"When a post becomes available..."*

After an hour they called me in
to express their disappointment
to tell me I seemed *Terribly dull*
And how they wished to appoint *interesting* people

I thought of the restless night and chill 4-30 start
the crowded train and walk through drizzle leaves and dogshit
my blurted incoherent answers

But more of weeks spent bickering, smouldering provocation
Flung half read novels and pointed silences
Her angry sighs of boredom

Well at least now it was official

Daybreak Lauds

Te Deum: The oral tradition

Yet others too are wakeful
Finally solace in birdsong

Paeans to brightness
to glorify their gods
or does instinct free from all happiness
all rage
       For all we know
these flutings may be outcries
the sobbing of the starved for the failed clutch
territory lost to the crow
through lengthening hours urgent calls
for the mate still not returned
and from the martin's nest
elegies for the chick clawed out by jays

In its shroud of thin white feather
I lifted scored flesh to bury or dispose in trash

Where the blackbird shatters shell on stone
there should be rituals delicate as the veined leaf
for grey light grown upon forest and street
in a language unwritten incomprehensible
and blameless
               Of this make song

First hour of daylight: Prime

I clear ash to lay fresh twigs
This year's fires burned low on screenshots
of contagion and trucks stacked with bodybags

A charred annulus of failed applewood calendars events
I count back the rings

year of a birth
a wedding
events in threes

But in Friar Daw I read of *fourre*
general synnes
seditions gluttony pride and
superstition
a word for that which stands above

Yeats knew when to make his will
I sweep last embers
                      the end of us

Ora pro nobis

In lime-sweet air and sun at your back
pass quickly to mountainous Clermont
and seek the shrine of Abraham
to rest among the high snows
for those who sleep at the tombs of saints are cured

Do not be afraid to leave
but remember as you travel
our thoughts in the dry riverbed
the dust of caves the fractured shell

Among your rediscoveries
possess the scented garden
the lily the quince
hedgerow and jasmine
juice of the grape and astringent olive
beneath the wheel of stars

know love's silences in the flight of owls

                                remember too
in the radiance of an unfamiliar light
those who wait beside the path of stones
brows marked with ash
that the shadow of Peter might cross their flesh

9 a.m. Terce

Watchkeeper

In my father's bureau my mother's watch
kept for outings
I test the bracelet I would stretch overhand upon her wrist

With a lifelong dread of keeping others waiting
she kept prompt to
buses meetings hospital appointments

and in the end left early

Commute

On reflection

Stalled in traffic
in the rear view mirror of the car in front
I catch eyes
looking forward but seeing back

and quickly away
from our mutual guilty shock.
That feeling-
Not going anywhere whichever way we looked
and waiting to move on

Being separate and unknowable
or as good as
meant secretive glances
to see if we were still looking
while avoiding contact

Waiting for anything to happen

Noon   Sext

natural charm

Today we unearth roots
clear bracken
consider options

Your rump among the borders
flower girl bent to weeding
straightens to press away the ache

At this hour all heads crane to the zenith
Dung and compost urge leaf and flower
On church porches or hidden under misericords
the green man's rictus spouts foliage
hedging our bets

Cattle chew the cud
Granaries fill
Dusty figures test the breeze
prepare sacks and unfurl sails
take the air at doors of creaking mills
calculate profit

In pubs laughter froths beer and pots of ale
Crumbs of bread and cheese are brushed aside
for cards and dominos

Did we share concern for how wheat ripened
sinews tautening at the press
for quarts of cider downed at the foot of haystacks
We lack leather gaiters and fiddle music
Where insects bloomed is emptied air and echoes
The ache in the muscle a memory of the flail

Now sweat leaks from your brow
You're stiff backed sluicing at the tap
Dirt under your nails will not come clean

Will there be rain tonight
Squinting to gauge the lean of shadow

If that's the time it's downhill from here

A leaf from Robert Herrick

In the garden I take instruction.
this is your domain
safer when I find the plant I have nurtured all week
is a weed

and must retrieve from the compost
a long prized specimen
Other errors I hastily cover
but you display an unerring instinct for guilt

Some dark secrets remain buried
behind the potting shed
I stick to watering leaf gathering
and avoid the mystery of seeds

Your deft fingers dispense largesse of bone meal
and advice is exact when it comes to pruning
I begin to learn to distinguish bramble
from the true stock

But we are making progress
In reclaiming territory the days develop a rhythm
and this early summer is a blessing
We have not worked together like this for years

Seeing you bend to tasks
and your bare shoulders gain the longed-for tan
I could regret much
about time not spent like this with you

recalling a phrase from a yellowed page
in one of those old books
I spend too much time reading
                                      Something about rosebuds

wild geese

that I would know the purposes of the wild geese
that certain things may come to pass
to follow their flight's strangeness is a skein of love
reforming secret and invisible pathways

remember how the ancients were visited by gods
now in their bodies' urge we witness grey ghosts
changing formation over the ploughland
each wingbeat a drive into consequence

I cannot tell you more than this
returning to a full and shifting gaze on landscapes
feeling the chill air and seeing something pass
that is neither instinct nor reason
our clasped fingers are a pattern
requiring no explanation no excuse

3 p.m.   Nones

Bad husbandry

Every year gales strip the branch
or birds foul green skin with short stabs
Brown wounds ferment juice

We never spot them before the rot sets in
dark suited Mafiosi leaving threats for us to find
Do we need to explain

Too soon means sour gobbets of white flesh at our feet
Too late and they are fallers
into damp grass where the slow worm coils

Let this year be a harvest
between the bitterness and the bruise

One way to find out
                            We reach up

madamimadam

When Adam took the second bite
was he less concerned than we think
about being evicted from Eden
After all with the loss of innocence he now had lust to console him
looking with narrowing eyes at Eve's breasts
and that interesting cleft between her legs
no longer just to generate the species
but a new form of entertainment
The next time Eve turned her back he went ahead anyway

And that's how it's been
a double benefit
reaching out applewards and at the same time
passing on the blame
Since then we've been beside ourselves

The woman made me do it

Anyway eventually someone may come along to save us

Maybe we shouldn't be too hard on our created creator
for immediately banging an eviction order
on the gate of our first parents
flaming sword and all
as the price of free will
After all He never had a choice
Who knows better what it means to endure something never asked for
to be an outsider constantly unequalled
with eternity to look forward to
alone among
thrones powers angels

diet of worms

on still life

keeping its distance
the blackbird's yellow beak stretches the worm's pink length
apparently we are more acutely aware of nature

Not everything in the garden is lovely
hens' feet rot in chicken farms
and toads crawl out from stones to gulp down slugs
In isolation lies security

We are learning still life
from this window I watch an empty street
enjoy occasional birdsong
make soup from vegetables on the turn
hear the rattle of lorries bringing bread and milk to shops
and throughout the day sirens
as ambulances ferry the dying to the back of the queue

After our reformation who will be called to account
the toppling of statues is not enough
will history be replaced merely by absence and silence

after all this is more comfortable
this is after all still life

my window lights up
as through the night tractors haul trailer loads of the third cut of silage
my diet is better than most of the world

friends say be positive
we clapped for nurses
things may change

but I am haunted by the question
for whom was that reminder the Old Masters always painted
into each still life
tucked away at the edge of the bowl
gnawing to the core
the curling worm

News from Lesbos

Does kindness mean buying the Big Issue
cutting a neighbour's grass
delivering shopping
holding open a door
giving up your place in a queue
remembering birthdays

It should be more than this
like not giving up on someone
sharing a belief
or a meal
or a whole culture
-as if one could

But even all that does not seem enough for so large a word
—learning the sense of one's kind
one's whole nature

It may be in the sense of wonder at what people can still do
when they have lost everything
even the strength to crawl up onto a beach

In the news I hear from Lesbos
of people who wait to drag them
from the surf
with their backs to the sea that swallowed their children
find blankets bottles of water
and an offer of shelter

Even though many would call this kindness
this is common humanity
or penance

Kindness is harder because it seems more difficult
than duty or friendship
or loving your neighbour
It is in the hard things about yourself
like making a mistake you can never correct
and though its weight bears down more with the years
finding a way to begin to learn how to forgive yourself

in spite of yourself

To the maids in a time of danger

the hour of carnival
after perfume and rouge the mask
accessory for filtered breath
                                    fear the hot blood

night's promised entertainment
opera or ballet
offers death by arias or by dancing
                                    the best hope is to escape
notice

the wilful air on your cheek
the unwanted caress of strangers
a scalding
              after sad viols only thought is pure

aromatic herbs and plague doctors can't redeem
Jacobeans addressing skulls
rather solicit milk-white Galatea
                              guard the flesh from change

for this one cool evening
last torches spent we stand to watch
with Venus low and radiant
the trajectory of satellites
                           I would hold your hand

rumours leech pestilence
distort our narrative
laden tables await the worm
                              do not reach out

set the mind to benefits of isolation
persuade ourselves as virtue of denial
how sun ages skin
                          we are love's dark matter

remember how in prison Irina Ratushinskaya
committed to memory words she gouged into soap
and cleansed herself with poetry
                          in her tortured hours

a sainted maker
among the legends of good women
praised *bothe in this werke and in their sorwes alle*
                          bespeak her powers in solitude

in the frosts of the cell her *brigand forests*
as they beat her head against a trestle
how she summoned thoughts of friends
                          now pass quickly the unlit corner

to the door the room the mirror
the unclothing
before the print of Danae and the shower of gold

on her release she would learn how in the Hermitage
the features of that princess
were ravaged by the acid and the knife
                          though forbidden we still cherish proximity

where hedgerows breed red campion navigate the ruined causeway
among the sneers   the accusations
that breach our thin disguises
                          the fever of our shame

how in that dawn echoes from the passing wagons
the cries of lambs in shuttered layers
were voices of the dead
                          distant through the usurped domains

upon contaminated streets we have breathed secrets
close the ears to whispers   the heart to malice
erase the air's contagion
                          Rest among the errors of our ways

Sunset   Vespers

Canticle

Evening distils heartsease
and a blue dragonfly
a voice calling from the house
and a tractor working two fields away

Day's heat is over
Now late swifts will be casting black skeins over Garn Goch

Through smart of tears we scan imagined visitations
and burn out vision against the dipping sun
                                            The sword of flame

From your garden of herbs
crush flowers for tincture
bathe the sight

In a cairn on Fan Foel they uncovered three urns
of cremated remains
                        Before the fire
mourners strewed the bodies with meadowsweet
with prayers for appeasements
easement of pain
                        to which unhearing gods
then sanctified the ash with petals and scent
and turned away

Their grief is the silence when the wind stills
the cascade over stones
the rustle of leaves
the lingering touch on skin

Clouds refract red
                The age of miracles

At the first chill we turn to each other
from the shading of eyes
to pluck the wild strawberry
Dei Gratia
scent of jasmine

A mute contract in the hush of grasses
Here we have laboured

Before retiring   Compline

Even Song

Be ready, sings Manu from a garden in Spain
where vines droop in heat
He has no hope, only a smile that is infectious

Others with guitars take up his song
from rooftops and deserts and alleys of graffiti
away from the bullets

Be ready, sings Manu from a sunlit garden
passing it on
to drummers on dry plains

Be ready, sings Manu and plays out the hour
beating time into evening prayer
for those who live to outlive the day and endure the night

Among cool trees of the Appalachians
two girls sing out the need for joy
and the readiness for love

And in that urge of rhythm no-one misses a beat
though caught in the weeping
eternal and inescapable

Be ready they sing, and are:
for the first skin of ice on the river's flow,
the green bud, cast chrysalis, the uncurling leaf

To this music cattle will be fed,
goats herded, water carried, cassava pounded,
and children called from play

Manu knows only that he must bridge vastnesses
to achieve synchronicity
from this high walled garden

May all innocence be blessed but especially his,
In time and harmony across continents
memory of an evening among shadows from late sun

Piano piano...

Last light
Roosting birds settle final differences
until song fades

This was the hour for practice
a last duty before bed
when nocturnes soothed the house

Our daughters inherited your tenderness of touch-
notes sustained to aching silence
testing the weight of air

Sometimes I touch the keys for resonances
and try how night is formed of this warm dark
rustling of leaves and voices far off made perfect

and softenings and how memory works
the way silence like absence matters
holding out to futures

Colour drains from berry and branch
In the shortening of days a late sonata
The autumn garden poised for hardship

recalls the golden the flaxen haired
easing in measured ceremonies of the soul
that address to moonlight

I will make my peace with this

Finis

The Art of Prayer

Great Duke
was it the colours of the word you worshipped
love for its own sake of
the constantly reworked angels never far off
distraction of gorgeous ladies robed in purples and blues

Did radiance of the page more than prayer
become a secret indulgence

That word for forgiveness but also shame

Beneath the calibrations of constellations
among the visions of your great commission
do we share one thought
                            Did you
among the splendour of towers and forests and streams
and the humble glorified by the tilling of your fields
find one image to which you constantly returned
as I do
naked and tempted

and most dwell upon the fall of man

Light Airs

Orpheus in the underpass

morning handed with latte and laptop
but at evening she'd spin a coin
through streetwalkers routed back to Bank
and never missed
                      in the underpass
he'd change his tune
each outcast note to draw her back
through piss
graffiti and keeping left
on his cheek deep Central's pulsing breath
under lamps his tracking gaze
watched diminishings through yellow air
song fading with her passing thought
and phone's caress
                              later
steel shutters lock cheap jewellery away
he keeps echo's tenancy till midnight
secret among the dreaming dispossessed
then vibrant from a velvet case
shakes out bright gems where her stilettos passed

Fire on Saddleworth

first the insects
each blackened carapace a tiny Icarus
precursor to ash
a momentary loss
before the grasses' uplift yellows
to flame
and the fallow's scorch
reaches down through the peatland
to white bone's lodgements

beyond potency of the eye
spiralling larks
from atomised nests and charred shell
outstrip smoke's ascent
faint auguries
labouring towards song

Girl arranging bananas

you have an eye for this
a still life
stepping up at full stretch
to turn and favour shades
try new angles
find the light

I would have you take all life in hand
a treasury of ripeness
in considered arrangement
best side displayed
aware we bruise easily

The uses of avocado

in Eden such gnarled rind could never tempt
to undo flesh like no other
a weighed thought

from first taste's cool
a deep well
satisfactory and full of itself

a secret at pause
an opened astonishment
of essence and stone

mellow complexion
hinting Magdalene
never without spikenard

oxymoron of thick skinned tenderness
undressed
teaches not all experience is piquant

hollowed to a small bowl
of leathery skin
a serviceable craft for small beings

its smooth subtlety of flesh
in the wrong hands
a recipe for disaster

unsweet unsavoury
invents new definitions
for desire

or potted in sunlit windows
all innocence
an awakening

in a triptych of flesh too easily bruised
impenetrable core and self protection
a parable of survival

and a shelf life summons
narrating in shade and texture
an entirely green myth

of love as yet to be identified
a pallor and verdure
awaiting imprint

at midnight in secret pleasures
a singular presence
totally unlike

Inkling

that inkwell dipper a blunt stick
my left hand scrawl
blotting line by line

over my shoulder teachers tutted and
walked off shaking their heads
pondering lost causes

in latter years attempts at love letters
were all illegible
and necessarily
brief
    some would say curt
but not a word I would risk

affairs were short lived due to
miscommunication
wrong places times
misread intentions

I couldn't fathom how to navigate a page
without despoiling everything said and done

diaries were composed in shorthand hieroglyphs
impossible to reinterpret
so the past was lost under Rorschach blots

in the perfection of this dark art
crossing out became redundant

eventually it was a comfort to know
I could get along
obscuring as I go

like a snail trail in the morning
blurred evidence of laborious
apparently aimless progress
the perpetrator untraceable
                        in the end

inured to the prospect of never being clear
writing became a hardened habit
a shell-like refuge
            which is why
I can give reasons but not explain—please see above—
the fact that at your departure I did not convey
in perfect cursive hand
things I did not then—or now
feel free to say

Dawn chorus cadenza

shape shifters in grey light
improvise last dark
murmurations recycle sounds
from staves in crooks of boughs
artful galleries
and chorus lines
rounding on themselves

tuning up
the where-were-yous
street cries
domestics over concubines
hungover trade offs
palaverings
serious counsels over crusts

the claw's curl through lichen into bark
brightenings of the medium
on worm cast and leaf
fire coloratura from bell towers
guttering
ridge tile

rung changes
from copse to field
pylon and park
red brick
urn and patio
the urgent matter of song redefined

in their psalms
phrase by phrase a coming to terms
as dark's rumour flourishes
all go to ground though skies are wide
still in limitless scales
a joyful worthwhile

yet tell sweet passeri
is it free-fall notes that such constancies proclaim
or caught breath after echo vibrancies
at dawn's bright wave-break
fulsome promise
of light
more light
          keen air

Lammas

something is happening to the year
with leaves' first brittle edge
colder looks raised collars turned backs
time to seek a blessing

hlaf-mas loaf -mass
mid-point of solstice and equinox
feast of first harvest
meant rights to pasture   freedom to glean

we must relearn what we have forgotten
with Lammas bread
find a new ritual   an axis shift
for the sorrows of friends

between the stones hard-shelled seed
ricochets and shatters to bran
from gold falls fine dust
a whiteout

through which we trace names
make silent wishes
and knead their secret
into the warm fermentation of yeast

set aside one fertile nub of dough
a tiny outcast of hope
laid up for another future
a resilience

throughout the house make visitations
in each corner
lay aromatic herbs for healing
breathe them as we sleep

and when we have shuttered the dark
await day's proof of the work of hands
a close textured transfiguration
against the grain

Angelus

angelus is the last sky's waking
frost melt
counting waves against the quay

on the beach
sting of each grain's moment
unforgiving

watching the fishing boats return
the still living stream
silvering the wharves

words made flesh
night whispers torturer's sneer
whimper of the starved child

light incarnate
in the mirror
the weakening

blood calling to blood
passion in the dark hours
cannot sustain not fulfil

in the cities sound of traffic
glint of hotel windows
voices in hallways husks of flies

statues in the museum
broken things
half things

the slow account
of one clock ticking
pointing silence

what the waves carve
the dry host
the mind's nobility

cliffs' erosion
the blank sheet's whiteness
the hollowness of days

framing your picture in memory
incision scars
the red seamed flesh

on Pont des Arts
the shape of ruin
burdens too great

the settling of air
between each peal
not stillness not silence

unresting
the unspoken unforgotten
the yet unloved

the rustle of your dress
a prayer at nightfall
pale light on limbs

quickening of breath
the pulse in the thighs
the awaited unborn

from shimmering water
shifting reflections
across the bay lights receding

angelus is the last dawn's breaking
frost set
wave wash at tide's reach

within the shell
formed flesh bone hardening
to fabric of time

a calling to mind
the wind borne
the focused self

yellowing light on park benches
mothers intent and whispering
walking through leaves

muted sorrowings
the cry of birds
at nightfall

towards definitions
flame
ash

Presences

Ghosts are a habit of mind
Hardy saw it from his vista of bending boughs
and Wordsworth in the sear of absence
My friend you too will haunt me
at moments when I stand hunting out a certain book
or at pause searching for better words
        hearing a footfall in the next room
a door opening on birdsong
or by windows wide to green hills
on my cheek what feels like breath
or the smart of rain
Come the peripheral flick of shadow
I'll await that familiar gentle nudge
less importunate than affirmatory
an intercession
to move me
              in the right direction

The miller's tale

begins with the snood
donned for purposes practical and hygienic
to contain the fall of long hair
gathered at the back
                but mainly
accentuating the delicate nape of your neck

a loose hood framing the face
worn casually
so flour-whitened fingers may coax in
any recalcitrant tress

a new consignment means our home
though not manorial
stands readied
a motte and bailey against circumstance

soon hope will be tried and set to prove
overnight in gentle heat
                and we
of a certain age
can hunker down with our sack of spelt
start another bottle
and think how best to spend an autumn evening

tide mills filled with a slow ease of half a day's rising waters
then unleashed pent torrents
through axle beam gears and pulleys
to set tonnage of millstone spinning and spilling
delicate threads from their weight

overshot wheels
in diverted runnels and leats
shouldered the stream at their downturn
and from headrace to tailrace
made killing grounds for otters

post mills turned delicate vanes windward
feeling for light airs
tremors through the windshaft
but ground out the same perfections from grist

millers' thumbs grow square and squat
press-testing coarseness run from stone
so bakers could thrust a forearm in the sack
if the flour stuck the milling was right

to date no record has been discovered of deaths caused by bakers' sweat

in 1191 Abbot Samson of Bury St Edmunds
ordered the destruction of a windmill
built on glebe land without permission

but today we grind free of soke or suit of mill
without tide or wind
and learn decline
hastened by Black Death
and climatic variation
     we take heed
a fifth of the harvest of Egypt during the seven years of abundance

at three hundred feet
Llyn Brianne dam corrals the headwaters of the Tywi
its stone harvested and milled to size on site
three turbines generate 4.6 megawatts

the quarry faces over Rhandirmwyn
and behind the hill
Twm Sion Cati's cave where I crawled in once
to discover a slit of open sky and
walls of graffiti
    from further up the valley
near Soar y Mynydd chapel
came clay to seal the dam's shelving core
      Zoar the sanctuary
      of Lot and his daughters
      spared by God from fire and salt

in Kent a small victory
our daughter and her husband watch fields turn green then gold
spend a morning gleaning
all afternoon wrists ache at the quern
a whole day's labour
is sufficient to make
one hard crusted loaf

now dark settles with seed dust
we re-peg the sack against mites and mildew
in the kitchen I flip a switch and an armature spins
over your shoulder I watch you pour
for a wholegrain milling to bran and flour
like time running out
                        but that said
wise and virtuous maker
in yeast
and sweat
and water warmed to heat of blood
your hair falling loose
with whitened fingers bunched to kneading fists
lives determination that miracle still is feasible

a promise made in wine and bread

The molluscs on theology

there must be some mistake

we approach in the spirit of worship
through daylight cloistering in the invisible places
perfecting our orisons
that we may draw close to you at night

your brightnesses awe and terrify us

too humble openly to demonstrate our love
secretly until dawn we carve metaphors of praise into your brassicas
but you lay out salt to sear our skin

at first we assumed mere catastrophe
but constant recurrence
forces us to dismiss any possibility of natural disaster

we execute delicate trails in secretions of our essence
offering curled poems of praise to you

it seems you do not read them
but place blue pellets that rot us from the inside
until only thought is left

we die without hope in the absence of any sign
and without forgiveness for sins we do not recognise
in the frosts of the dark season we still our breath
and hope to wake again

faith tells us you do not consciously intend harm
that our suffering is part of some plan you alone comprehend
though the copper threads you stretch across our modest pathways
would turn others aside from loving intentions
we continue to martyr ourselves upon them

sometimes we are gathered tenderly
delicately prised from our divine offices
to be cast to wild creatures that devour us
in this land of sacrifice
in the light of such events our suspicions deepen

in spite of tests of faith we conduct our rituals with slow dignity
finding solace in our common history
but eventually may be compelled to confront our doubts
and direct our devotions
to more worthy gods

Light airs

a wetted finger held aloft prophesied rain or sun
but reading cloudscapes caught us out
false friends in rusted weathercocks on churches
faithless from traffic surge forest gust and hedgerow

just as bad the lift of leaves
or eyeing wind waves shift through wheat
red eyed daring ourselves not to blink
tracking the dust of it forced tears

when two fronts pile in
cloud laden from wide points on horizons
brewing slow cascades
bisect the angle to look for trouble

or on the Black Mountain
trace hawthorn skylined on the falling dark
a shriving racked by constants of prevailing wind
bent to circumstance they blacken and survive

where we stopped the car
white in headlights the v of ears spelt hare
ghosting across winter fields on serious business
at pause fur stippling and lifting

her pale flame through the valleys
nesting in heath grass almost homeless
asking in the frost's blue ache of stars
after such blessing why these tears

or memory of tresses in the breeze
the unenduring exorcism of desire
never to be trusted
hair blown back as she walks away

no
    the only sure method to compass air
is the way we kiss politely on the cheek
offering the profile to the faintest breath
tenderness is all where weeping falls

to get true bearings on what's to come
sense the coolness of its faint caress
like something almost no longer there

then turn and face it

Chopstick variations

settling to an evening's whittling
a boatman splits bamboo
works down to a smooth polish

for a sleepy emperor
in his gentle digestion he pardons crimes
and dreams greatly

do not transgress
kanzashi in a coquette's topknot
are not to be thought of

erect and inviting
sending blood coursing through passing strangers
now they will not sleep

never shared
respectfully borne close to the heart
but sociable essential

a moral figuring
this hand to mouth feeder of millions
where no grain must be lost

whose adept manipulation
if we are to succeed and thrive
must become art then instinct

so powers conceived
through hand heart eye
sustain the everyday

for food hard won is doubly blessed
skill and effort qualify senses
so mark this humble implement

and praise a democratic artistry
a practical Pythagorean collusion
whose finger thumb triangulation

requires concentration
and care over simple matters
We should make much of you in our meditations

ii
tonight once more we pour wine
settle plates and glasses light candles

and find words of reason and consolation
as dark settles on our contentment

with windows wide to summer
curtains stir with cool breaths of mountain air

news relates spreading forest fires
protesters with umbrellas mown down by water cannon

too little
too much

we hunch over a meal of rice
embarrassed amateurs mishandling chopsticks

poising gemlike seeds
of tiny precarious nourishment

and think

this is how half the world survives
sparingly grain by grain

we stain the cloth
should we choose can set our failings aside

but persevere
afraid to make light of our causes

iii
etiquette

never thrust upright in food
neither crossed nor wielded singly
acts echoing rites for the dead

also passing from stick to stick
is how the bones are handled
after a cremation

unmatching pairs and table drumbeats
are out of order
for hair accessories see above

wooden chopsticks rubbed together
implies poor quality
fear of splinters

sucking on or spearing
pointing or emphasis when holding forth
should be resisted

stir food with your stick
only if your intention
is insult to cooks

touch communal plates
specifically with serving chopsticks
pick up rice in manageable morsels

avoid indecision
hovering over too much choice
is vulgar and unnerving

so it seems wise to keep these items
at the back of a drawer
reminders brought out on occasions

that others do things differently
deserve care in our dealings
and are worthy of respect

Triple point

i.

new moon and the full tide's at pause
a forecast south westerly will sweep in the next storm
to fill culverts flood fields halt traffic

wind and current from Biscay will ram Eddystone
bludgeon up to Norwegian fjords and moraines
not a day for longships

this morning's transmissions interrupted
gale warnings on the hour every hour
diligent watchkeepers will have it mapped

with dividers on carefully laid out charts
nothing to be done   when it hits
it will be wind against tide

along the beach our prints point to the arctic
then quickening lengthen and veer for home
yours straight mine in short legged scallopings

and crossed before that handhold pause
as gulls scavenged at the wave reach slime
among salt stink net and weed scum

emptying for miles before the onslaught
this readying inbreath as we gather shells
at Mont Saint Michelle there are refuges for the negligent

but out here you're on your own
you won't outrun or negotiate with this
eventually your picked bones might wash up

heading for the car park kicking sand from our boots
behind us white horses even at this slack tide
a natural distribution curve means something always about to happen

the moon's grab a constant inevitability beyond even this variable
so attention is necessary   heed all warnings
know   like most things this is merely temporary   for now—
wait

ii

salt rimed icemen
or dried to leather under relentless suns
backed by tides strange mists

palms skinned   frozen to the oar
swollen tongued not knowing their own cries
in thirst crazed landfalls at dawn

the constants of raiding overwintering
starving for springs of pillage axed tonsures gold cups
murder of kings and broken treaties

does it come in the moment of wiping a sword
the heartleap of thought desire need
to sit at a hearth

to interrogate the language the line the form
and balance the point where idea catches breath
as in the account of the *micel here*

as Asser tells it   almost indifferently
recording that there is also profit for a people
to toil the plough-land and support themselves

iii

tonight our breath makes ghosts in the cold room
our mist leaves messages on glass's interface with zero
where a finger's warmth will start a river

we stack books on shelves
arrange shells
try to make connections

outside frost has intentions on stiffening grass
on black boughs birds know what's coming
grow silent feathering out in a waiting game

of who will make the grey dawn
by starlight they eye who is marked
for the day that will not come

against the sear of cold sheets our mutual clutch
for stolen heat feels like cheating
but after all this is a kind of sharing

we will cast breakfast crusts on the paths
stiff feathers found in the chill
will hasten us chasten us now touch is rarer

to remember in tomorrow's expansive air
if what streams down the panes makes us think of tears
while we return the same among altered things

We let love breathe

To learn

The accurate identification of garden birds
Tide tables
The geography of undiscovered countries
their shorelines creeks and atolls
the prediction of their storms and awe among their cataracts
Star charts and rules of navigation
for traversing the loneliness of crowds
Whether artichokes were successfully cultivated in ancient Egypt
The strangeness of sun on garden walls
Patience
Why there are so many unread books on my shelves
The private affairs of my neighbours
The weight of footfalls of small creatures
Siege warfare and the advantages of wooden horses
The cartography of the path to salvation
In the science and interpretation of Japanese windbells
the significance of cherry blossom
Acceptance of love's mutability
(difficult)
Its transgressions and forgiveness
Why I dream of certain people at uncertain times
The true colour of the eyes of the beloved
The thoughtful arrangement of terra cotta on Parisian balconies
The acquisition of visionary powers
and the ability in summer to consume ice cream before it melts
A seriousness of purpose
The simple line

Lightning Source UK Ltd.
Milton Keynes UK
UKHW012015110521
383548UK00001B/86